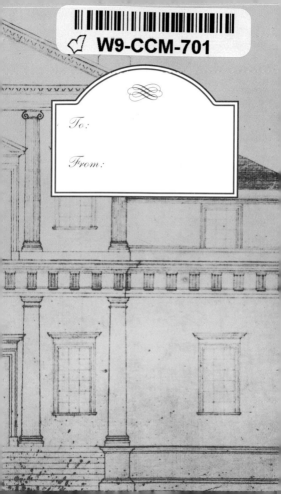

To:

From:

Thomas JEFFERSON

H<u>is W</u>or<u>ds</u>
AND
V<u>isi</u>on

Edited by Nick Beilenson

Photographs from Corbis-Bettmann Collection

PETER PAUPER PRESS, INC.
WHITE PLAINS, NEW YORK

For Evelyn

All photographs are from Corbis-Bettmann,
902 Broadway, New York, NY 10010

Endpapers: Architect's drawing of
Jefferson's home at Monticello, VA
Page 8: Black & white copy of the
Rembrandt Peale painting acquired by
Jacqueline Kennedy for the White House
Page 14: Portrait by Jon Trumbull
Page 18: Portrait by Rembrandt Peale
Page 31: Portrait by Rembrandt Peale
Page 38: Portrait by C.W. Peale

Visit us at www.peterpauper.com

TABLE OF CONTENTS

INTRODUCTION

*I have sworn upon the altar
of God eternal hostility
against every form of tyranny
over the mind of man.*

Thomas Jefferson, born in Virginia in
1743, lived in an age of revolution
and emerging democracy. Through
his ideas and active service as a statesman, he, more than any other
American, placed his stamp on that
democratic experiment, the United
States of America.

Jefferson served from 1769-76 in the
Virginia House of Burgesses. He
attended the Continental Congress in
Philadelphia in 1775-76 and was from
1776-79 a member of the Virginia

House of Delegates. He served one term as Governor of Virginia (and was almost captured by the British as they drove through Charlottesville and his mountaintop estate at Monticello). Jefferson served as Minister to France from 1785-89 and as Secretary of State under President Washington from 1790-93.

A candidate for president, Jefferson was elected vice-president in 1796. In 1800 he again ran for president, and, after political maneuvering brought on by the fact that he and his running mate Aaron Burr received the same number of votes in the electoral college, he was elected by the House of Representatives in 1801 as third president of the United States. Jefferson served two terms as president and then retired in 1809 to his beloved

Monticello. During his retirement, he oversaw his estate, kept up a monumental correspondence (he wrote over 15,000 letters during his lifetime), and founded the University of Virginia at nearby Charlottesville. He died on July 4, 1826, at the age of 83.

Jefferson played a crucial role in the Revolutionary Era not only as statesman and politician but through his seminal writings, political documents firmly based on the philosophical doctrine of the law of nature. His 1774 *Summary View of the Rights of British America*, which declared that "the British parliament has no right to exercise authority over us," brought Jefferson to the attention of two continents. Two years later, he drafted the Declaration of Independence, and in 1777 he

drafted the Virginia Bill for Establishing Religious Freedom which called for political equality for all citizens regardless of their religion or lack of it.

Jefferson was not only a statesman and politician. He was a lawyer, educator, mathematician, surveyor, philosopher, scientist, architect, geographer, philologist, and musician. President John F. Kennedy truly had reason to say to a group of Nobel Laureates: "I think that this is the most extraordinary collection of talent, of human knowledge, that has ever gathered together at the White House, with the possible exception of when Thomas Jefferson dined alone."

N. B.

THE JEFFERSON MEMORIAL

The words that follow,
reflecting Thomas Jefferson's
most important principles,
are inscribed on four
panels on the walls of the
Jefferson Memorial in
Washington, D.C.

First Panel: Declaration of Independence

We hold these truths to be self-evident: that all men are created equal, that they are endowed by their Creator with certain inalienable rights, among these are life, liberty and the pursuit of happiness, that to secure these rights governments are instituted among men. We . . . solemnly publish and declare, that these colonies are and of right ought to be free and independent states . . . And for the support of this declaration, with a firm reliance on the protection of divine providence, we mutually pledge our lives, our fortunes, and our sacred honour.

Second Panel: Religious Freedom

Almighty God hath created the mind free. All attempts to influence it by temporal punishments or burthens . . . are a departure from the plan of the Holy Author of our religion . . . No man shall be compelled to frequent or support any religious worship or ministry or shall otherwise suffer on account of his religious opinions or belief, but all men shall be free to profess and by argument to maintain, their opinions in matters of religion. I know but one code of morality for men whether acting singly or collectively.

Third Panel: Slavery/Education

God who gave us life gave us liberty. Can the liberties of a nation be secure when we have removed a conviction that these liberties are the gift of God? Indeed I tremble for my country when I reflect that God is just, that his justice cannot sleep forever. Commerce between master and slave is despotism. Nothing is more certainly written in the book of fate than that these people are to be free. Establish the law for educating the common people. This it is the business of the state to effect and on a general plan.

Fourth Panel: Constitution and Laws

I am not an advocate for frequent changes in laws and constitutions, but laws and institutions must go hand in hand with the progress of the human mind. As that becomes more developed, more enlightened, as new discoveries are made, new truths discovered and manners and opinions change, with the change of circumstances, institutions must advance also to keep pace with the times. We might as well require a man to wear still the coat which fitted him when a boy as civilized society to remain ever under the regimen of their barbarous ancestors.

JEFFERSON THE DEMOCRAT

*Jefferson, the patrician landowner,
lived in and reflected an age
of revolution and democracy.*

✯ The Constitution of the United States is the result of the collected wisdom of our country.
        [1801 Letter to Amos Marsh]

✯ What signify a few lives lost in a century or two? The tree of liberty must be refreshed from time to time with the blood of patriots & tyrants. It is its natural manure.
            *[1787 Letter from Paris
                to William S. Smith]*

✶ A wise and frugal government, which shall restrain men from injuring one another, shall leave them otherwise free to regulate their own pursuits of industry and improvement, and shall not take from the mouth of labor the bread it has earned.

✶ Were it left to me to decide whether we should have a government without newspapers, or newspapers without government, I should not hesitate a moment to prefer the latter. But I should mean that every man . . . be capable of reading them.

[1787 Letter to Edward Carrington]

✼ I consider the people who constitute a society or nation as the source of all authority in that nation.

[Opinion on the French Treaties, 1793]

✼ The disease of liberty is catching.

[1820 Letter to Lafayette]

✼ With all the imperfections of our present government, it is without comparison the best existing or that ever did exist.

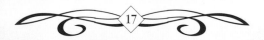

JEFFERSON ON PUBLIC POLICY

Jefferson believed in a government of laws and not of men, of separation of powers, and in states' rights.

✫ It would be a dangerous delusion were a confidence in the men of our choice to silence our fears for the safety of our rights: that confidence is everywhere the parent of despotism—free government is founded on jealousy, and not in confidence; it is jealousy and not confidence which prescribes limited constitutions ... In questions of power, then, let no more

be heard of confidence in man, but bind him down from mischief by the chains of the Constitution.

[Kentucky Resolutions, 1798]

✶ The Legislative, Executive and Judiciary offices shall be kept for ever separate, & no person exercising the one shall be capable of appointment to the others, or to either of them. . . .

Every person of full age neither owning nor having owned [50] acres of land, shall be entitled to an appropriation of [50] acres or to so much as shall make up (a full 50 acres) . . .

[Draft Constitution for Virginia, 1776]

★ *Resolved*, That the several States composing the United States of America; are not united on the principle of unlimited submission to their General Government; but that, by a compact under the style and title of a Constitution for the United States, and of amendments thereto, they constituted a General Government for special purposes, delegated to that government certain definite powers, reserving, each State to itself, the residuary mass of right to their own self-government; and that whensoever the General Government assumes undelegated powers, its acts are unauthoritative, void, and of no force . . .

[Kentucky Resolutions]

✶ Unless the President's mind on a view of everything which is urged for and against this bill [for the establishment of a National Bank], is tolerably clear that it is unauthorised by the Constitution; if the pro and the con hang so even as to balance his judgment, a just respect for the wisdom of the legislature would naturally decide the balance in favor of their opinion. It is chiefly for cases where they are clearly misled by error, ambition, or interest, that the Constitution has placed a check in the negative of the President.

[Opinion on the Constitutionality of a National Bank, 1791]

★ The remaining revenue on the consumption of foreign articles, is paid cheerfully by those who can afford to add foreign luxuries to domestic comforts, being collected on our seaboards and frontiers only, and incorporated with the transactions of our mercantile citizens, it may be the pleasure and pride of an American to ask, what farmer, what mechanic, what laborer, ever sees a tax-gatherer of the United States?

[Second Inaugural Address, 1805]

✯ During this course of administration, and in order to disturb it, the artillery of the press has been levelled against us, charged with whatsoever its licentiousness could devise or dare. These abuses of an institution so important to freedom and science, are deeply to be regretted, inasmuch as they tend to lessen its usefulness, and to sap its safety . . .

. . . since truth and reason have maintained their ground against false opinions in league with false facts, the press, confined to truth, needs no other legal restraint; the public judgment will correct false reasonings and opinions, on a full hearing of all parties . . .

[Second Inaugural Address]

The house in which Thomas Jefferson wrote the Declaration of Independence, Philadelphia, Pennsylvania (undated illustration)

⭐ When we consider that this government is charged with the external and mutual relations only of these states; that the states themselves have principal care of our persons, our property, and our reputation, constituting the great field of human concerns, we may well doubt whether our organization is not too complicated, too expensive; whether offices and officers have not been multiplied unnecessarily, and sometimes injuriously to the service they were meant to promote.

*[First Annual Message
to Congress, 1801]*

✻ Our first and fundamental maxim should be, never to entangle ourselves in the broils of Europe. Our second, never to suffer Europe to intermeddle with cis-Atlantic affairs. America, North and South, has a set of interests distinct from those of Europe, and peculiarly her own. She should therefore have a system of her own, separate and apart from that of Europe.

[The Monroe Doctrine—1823 Letter to President James Monroe]

✶ Do we wish to acquire to our own confederacy any one or more of the Spanish provinces? I candidly confess, that I have ever looked on Cuba as the most interesting addition which could ever be made to our system of States.

[1823 Letter to President James Monroe]

✶ (A Bill of Rights) would help create a national sentiment to 'counteract the impulses of interest and passion' of popular majorities and provide a rallying point against a usurping government.

✶ Some men look at constitutions with sanctimonious reverence, and deem them like the ark of the covenant, too sacred to be touched. They ascribe to the men of the preceding age a wisdom more than human, and suppose what they did to be beyond amendment. I knew that age well; I belonged to it, and labored with it. . . . But I know also, that laws and institutions must go hand in hand with the progress of the human mind. As that becomes more developed, more enlightened, as new discoveries are made, new truths disclosed, and manners and opinions change with the change of circumstances, institutions must advance also, and keep pace with the times.

[1816 Letter to Samuel Kercheval]

✯ I cannot omit recommending a revisal of the laws on the subject of naturalization. . . . shall we refuse the unhappy fugitives from distress that hospitality which the savages of the wilderness extended to our fathers arriving in this land? Shall oppressed humanity find no asylum on this globe?

[First Annual Message to Congress]

✳ I have ever thought religion a concern purely between our God and our consciences, for which we were accountable to him, and not to the priests. I never told my own religion, nor scrutinized that of another. I never attempted to make a convert, nor wished to change another's creed. I have ever judged of the religion of others by their lives . . . For it is in our lives, and not from our words, that our religion must be read.

[1816 Letter to
Mrs. Samuel H. Smith]

✳ Compulsion in religion is distinguished peculiarly from compulsion

JEFFERSON ON RELIGION AND MORAL LAW

*Jefferson considered himself
a Christian, but had little use
for much of the clergy. Outside
the edifice of government
should stand a "wall"
between it and religion.*

✶ I am a *real Christian*, that is to say,
a disciple of the doctrines of Jesus,
very different from the Platonists,
who call *me* infidel and *themselves*
Christians and preachers of the
gospel, while they draw all their
characteristic dogmas from what its
author never said nor saw. They have

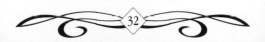

compounded from the heathen mysteries a system beyond the comprehension of man, of which (Jesus), were he to return on earth, would not recognize one feature.

[1816 Letter to Charles Thomson]

★ The doctrines of Jesus are simple, and tend all to the happiness of man. 1. That there is only one God, and he all perfect. 2. That there is a future state of rewards and punishments. 3. That to love God with all thy heart and thy neighbor as thyself, is the sum of religion.

*[1822 Letter to
Dr. Benjamin Waterhouse]*

✴ I have ever thought religion a
concern purely between our God
and our consciences, for which we
were accountable to him, and not to
the priests. I never told my own
religion, nor scrutinized that of
another. I never attempted to make a
convert, nor wished to change
another's creed. I have ever judged
of the religion of others by their
lives . . . For it is in our lives, and
not from our words, that our religion
must be read.

[1816 Letter to
Mrs. Samuel H. Smith]

✴ Compulsion in religion is distinguished peculiarly from compulsion

in every other thing. I may grow rich by an act I am compelled to follow, I may recover health by medicines I am compelled to take against my own judgment, but I cannot be saved by worship I disbelieve and abhor.

✴ [I regret that the Jewish sect] parent and basis of all those of Christendom [has been singled out by Christians] for a persecution and oppression which proved they have profited nothing from the benevolent doctrines of him whom they profess to make the model of their principles and practice.

[1820 Letter to Joseph Marx]

✴ *We, the General Assembly of Virginia do enact* that no man shall be compelled to frequent or support any religious worship, place, or ministry whatsoever, nor shall be enforced, restrained, molested, or burthened in his body or goods, nor shall otherwise suffer, on account of his religious opinions or belief; but that all men shall be free to profess, and by argument to maintain, their opinions in matters of religion, and that the same shall in no wise diminish, enlarge, or affect their civil capacities.

[Jefferson's 1777 Draft Bill for Establishing Religious Freedom]

✮ My opinion is that there would never have been an infidel, if there had never been a priest. The artificial structures they have built on the purest of all moral systems, for the purpose of deriving from it pence and power, revolts those who think for themselves, and who read in that system only what is really there.

[1816 Letter to Mrs. S. H. Smith]

✮ If you find reason to believe there is a god, a consciousness that you are acting under his eye, and that he approves you, will be a vast additional incitement. . . . if that Jesus was also a god, you will be comforted by a belief of his aid and love.

[1787 Letter to Nephew Peter Carr]

JEFFERSON THE MAN

*In his letters Jefferson gossiped,
grieved, praised marriage,
gave advice, and defined
happiness. He loved music. He
had a strong moral sense.
He felt himself to be a private
man, a scientist, who had been
led by events into
public service.*

✫ If there is any news stirring in
town or country, such as deaths,
courtships, or marriages, in the circle
of my acquaintance, let me know it.
Remember me affectionately to all
the young ladies of my acquaintance,

particularly the Miss Burwells, and Miss Potters, and tell them that though that heavy earthly part of me, my body, be absent, the better half of me, my soul, is ever with them; and that my best wishes shall ever attend them.

[1762 Letter to John Page]

✯ Health is the first requisite after morality.

[1787 Letter to Peter Carr]

✯ With respect to the distribution of your time the following is what I should approve.

from 8. to 10 o'clock practise music.

from 10. to 1. dance one day and
    draw another

from 1. to 2. draw on the day you
    dance, and write a letter the
    next day.

from 3. to 4. read French

from 4. to 5. exercise yourself in
    music.

from 5. till bedtime read English,
    write &c.

. . . If you love me then, strive to be
good under every situation and to all
living creatures, and to acquire those
accomplishments which I have put in
your power . . .

[1783 Letter to Daughter Martha,
age 11!]

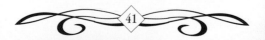

✷ Harmony in the married state is
the very first object to be aimed at.
The happiness of the domestic fire-
side is the first boon of Heaven.

✷ It is your future happiness which
interests me, and nothing can con-
tribute more to it (moral rectitude
always excepted) than the contracting
a habit of industry and activity. Of all
the cankers of human happiness
nothing corrodes with so silent, yet
so baneful a tooth, as indolence.
Body and mind, both unemployed,
our being becomes a burden, and
every object about us loathesome,

*Enlarging Glass in the possession
of Thomas Jefferson*

even the dearest . . . Exercise and application produce order in our affairs, health of body, cheerfulness of mind, and these make us precious to our friends. . . . [if] you catch yourself in idleness, start from it as you would from the precipice of a gulf. You are not, however, to consider yourself as unemployed while taking exercise. This is necessary for your health.

[1787 Letter to Martha Jefferson, at age 15]

✫ The glow of one warm thought is to me worth more than money.

✶ If there is a gratification which I envy any people in this world it is to [Italy] its music. This is the favorite passion of my soul, and fortune has cast my lot in a country where it is in a state of deplorable barbarism.

[1787 Letter to Giovanni Fabbroni]

✶ Within a few days I retire to my family, my books and farms; and having gained the harbor myself, I shall look on my friends still buffeting the storm, with anxiety indeed, but not with envy. Never did a prisoner, released from his chains, feel such

relief as I shall on shaking off the shackles of power. Nature intended me for the tranquil pursuits of science, by rendering them my supreme delight. But the enormities of the times in which I have lived, have forced me to take a part in resisting them, and to commit myself on the boisterous ocean of political passions.

*[1809 Letter to
P. S. Dupont de Nemours]*

✳ I find as I grow older that I love those most whom I loved first.

*Mr. Thomas Jefferson's pantograph,
not invented by him, but on which he
made suggestions for improvement*

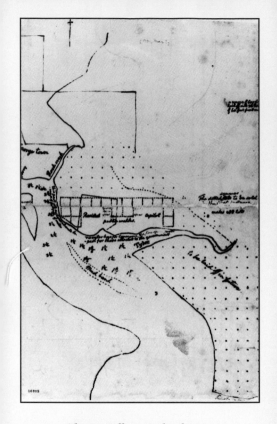

*Thomas Jefferson's sketch map
of Washington D.C. 1791*

JEFFERSON THE OBSERVER

*Jefferson held keen and
sometimes witty views on most
all subjects, including youth
and age, books and printing,
disputation, the American
character, travel, lawyers,
George Washington,
and Great Britain.*

✯ It is while we are young that the
habit of industry is formed. If not
then, it never is afterwards. The fortune of our lives, therefore, depends
on employing well the short period
of youth.

✯ It is objected . . . that he is 77
years of age [too old for public
office]; but at a much more advanced
age, our Franklin was the ornament
of human nature. He may not be able
to perform, in person, all the details
of his office; but if he gives us the
benefit of his understanding, his
integrity, his watchfulness, and takes
care that all the details are well per-
formed by himself or his necessary
assistants, all public purposes will be
answered.

*[1801 Letter to Elias Shipman and
Others, a Committee of the
Merchants of New Haven]*

✯ Books constitute capital. A library book lasts as long as a house, for hundreds of years. It is not an article of mere consumption but fairly of capital, and often in the case of professional men, setting out in life, it is their only capital.

[1821 Letter to James Madison]

✯ I have often thought that nothing would do more extensive good at small expense than the establishment of a small circulating library in every county . . .

[1809 Letter to John Wyche]

✭ I have now been thirty years avail-
ing myself of every possible opportu-
nity of procuring Indian vocabularies
to the same set of words . . .

[1809 Letter to
Dr. Benjamin S. Barton]

✭ The learning of Greek and Latin, I
am told, is going into disuse in
Europe. I know not what their manners and occupations may call for:
but it would be very ill-judged in us
to follow their example in this
instance.

[Notes on the
State of Virginia, 1781]

Thomas Jefferson's traveling liquor cabinet

✶ When I hear another express an opinion, which is not mine, I say to myself, He has a right to his opinion, as I to mine; why should I question it. His error does me no injury . . . If a fact be misstated, it is probable he is gratified by a belief of it, and I have no right to deprive him of the gratification. If he wants information he will ask it, and then I will give it in measured terms; but if he still believes his own story, and shows a desire to dispute the fact with me, I hear him and say nothing. It is his affair, not mine, if he prefers error.

[1808 Letter to Thomas Jefferson Randolph]

✯ The spirit of manufacture has taken deep root among us . . .

[1809 Letter to P. S. Dupont de Nemours]

✯ No duty the Executive had to perform was so trying as to put the right man in the right place.

✯ If the present [Continental] Congress errs in too much talking, how can it be otherwise, in a body to which the people send one hundred and fifty lawyers, whose trade it is to question everything, yield nothing, and talk by the hour?

[Autobiography, 1821]

★ I think I knew General Washington intimately and thoroughly . . . His mind was great and powerful, without being of the first order; . . . no judgment was ever sounder. It was slow in operation, being little aided by invention or imagination, but sure in conclusion . . . He was incapable of fear, meeting personal dangers with the calmest unconcern. Perhaps the strongest feature in his character was prudence . . . He was . . . a wise, a good, and a great man . . . His person, you know, was fine, his stature exactly what he would wish, his deportment easy, erect and noble; the best horseman of his age, and the most graceful

figure that could be seen on horseback.

> *[1814 Letter to Dr. Walter Jones]*

☆ A Tory has been properly defined to be a traitor in thought but not in deed.

☆ In Great-Britain it is said their constitution relies on the house of commons for honesty, and the lords for wisdom; which would be a national reliance if honesty were to be bought with money, and if wisdom were hereditary.

> *[Notes on the State of Virginia]*

✴ I fancy it must be the quantity of animal food eaten by the English which renders their character insusceptible of civilisation. I suspect it is in their kitchens and not in their churches that their reformation must be worked, and that Missionaries of that description from hence would avail more than those who should endeavor to tame them by precepts of religion or philosophy.

[1785 Letter from Paris
to Abigail Adams]

✴ I have seen enough of political honors to know that they are but splendid torments.

[1797 Letter to
Martha Jefferson Randolph]

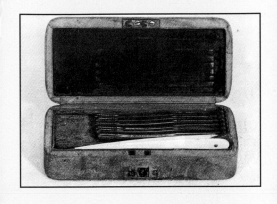

Thomas Jefferson's set of shaving knives

✶ No occupation is so delightful to me as the culture of the earth, and no culture comparable to that of the garden.
[1811 Letter to Charles Wilson Peale]

✶ I steer my bark with Hope in the head, leaving Fear astern.
[1816 Letter to John Adams]

✶ The boys of the rising generation are to be the men of the next, and the sole guardian of the principles we deliver over to them.

★ Whenever a man has cast a longing eye on them [public offices], a rottenness begins in his conduct.

[1799 Letter to Tench Coxe]

★ It is a part of the American character to consider nothing as desperate; to surmount every difficulty by resolution and contrivance.

★ This I hope will be the age of experiments in government, and that their basis will be founded on principles of honesty, not of mere force.

[1796 Letter to John Adams]

JEFFERSON'S LEGACY

✶ I carry with me the consolation of a firm persuasion that Heaven has in store for our beloved country long ages to come of prosperity and happiness. *[8th Annual Message to Congress, 1808]*

✶ My confidence in my countrymen generally leaves me without much fear for the future.

✶ Of you, then, my neighbors, I may ask, in the face of the world, "whose ox have I taken, or whom have I defrauded? Whom have I oppressed, or of whose hand have I received a bribe to blind mine eyes therewith?" On your verdict I rest with conscious security.

The third president of the United States, governor of Virginia, secretary of state and holder of many legislative offices wrote the following words to memorialize the actions for which he wished to be remembered:

Here was Buried
THOMAS JEFFERSON
Author of the
Declaration
of
American Independence
of the
Statute of Virginia
for
Religious Freedom
and Father of the
University of Virginia

These words appear on the gray granite obelisk marking his tomb in the family cemetery at Monticello.

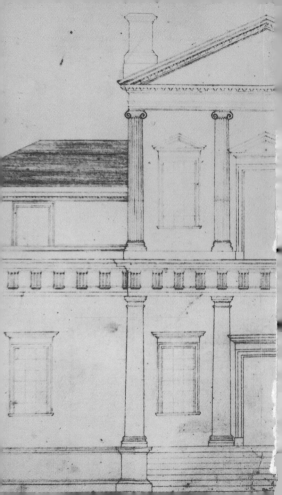